YOU'RE NOT ALONE

Layla Undine

A collection of poems written on a psychiatric ward

Typeset in Adobe Jenson Pro

Editing, design, typesetting and publishing by UK Book Publishing

www.ukbookpublishing.com

ISBN: 978-1-913179-70-0

ACKNOWLEDGEMENTS

Thank you to my Guardian Angel Joey for always
being there for me and answering my prayers.

Thanks to my Nan and Grandad, for making this
book and the books to follow possible.

I am grateful to all my fans out there that take their
time to buy and read my work – it means a lot.

Shay from St Andrews, Birmingham, thank you for saving my life.

Thank you to all my friends for supporting me in getting this far.

To my family, I love you for everything that you do for me.

And of course – without doubt – thank you again to all
at UK Book Publishing. You guys are diamonds!

YOU'RE NOT ALONE

A.B.B.A

You should never fall in love
And stop those suicide attempts
Everything has a consequence
There's nothing you should trust

Men are driven by their dicks
Women just want your money
Your friends are there 'til you have nothing
Yet I still fall for it

I'm a danger to myself
I'm either self-harming or letting others hurt me
I know that it's not worth it
But trouble is what I do best

Yesterday the sun was out
It was miserable for all of today
I had a tribunal that again I failed
So the weather matched my mood

I'm tired, leave me alone
I'm only writing this to pass the time
You know I like to play with rhymes
Go away, don't text or phone

ACHIEVER

I never really longed for fame
Until I realized how good it felt
That very first time I saw my name
All over the internet

I'm not exactly desperate
So long as I'm good at what I do
I've never had so many friends
And they all inspire me too

Standing up and shaking hands
"Could you please sign my book?"
Bless all of my steadfast fans
This is why I'll never give up

John Lennon at every concert would say
"Some people say I'm a dreamer"
I worked my arse off and despite delays
I'm happy to call myself an achiever

Tell yourself "We can do it too" and "You're not alone"
It all makes sense in the end
Indulge yourself, there's more to come
I'll never be stunted again

Whether you want to be a PM or an astronaut
A dancer or a doctor
There's space for all of us in this world
Just try that littler bit harder

CAN'T STAND TO HEAR YOU LAUGH

That giggle, that smile, those tears of happiness. It's not me that caused them, somebody else has taken my place and it would only be adult to wish the best for you but I can't. The jealousy burns through my skin and my blood boils with such hatred as I can't stand to see you laugh now we've been separated. I wanted you to suffer, to regret, to despise yourself for the way you treated me in which was the reason I left you. But it didn't happen. I guess you're better off without me...

CLOUDS

Like watching a slow movie
The earth is moving
Now and then I'll see a bird
Or is it a plane?
Wait – superman?
Anyway
Back to the candy floss in the sky
I can only see it
So long as the sun doesn't rule it
Kind of annoying
They block the chance of viewing
Another planet
Stars hide behind these clouds
As does the sun
And the moon
Monotonous in speed
But never in shape
Us English crave
For the sky to be blue
Then all we moan about is the heat
Typical
Still, it meditates me
Good therapy
I want to close my eyes
But I'm hypnotized
I lose track of time
Nothing matters
So long as I have the power to see
These beautiful clouds above me
(Until it rains)

DANDRUFF

I went out on leave with some money to spend
Then thought it would be nice to pamper myself
I decided to have sewn in a Caribbean weave
But man, it itches underneath
Two weeks later, my scalp is full of dandruff
Pissed off, I am – that hairstyle left me bankrupt!
It took a whole four hours to complete
Just sat in the mirror whilst my arse starts to ache
Look at me – I'm even scratching it now
All this shit for over two hundred pounds
Let me tell you it's not easy to manage
Well, at least I made a now wealthy hairdresser happy

DON'T WANT TO WORK

I don't want to work today
24 hours of doing fuck all
Leaving my underwear on the floor
Socks hanging half-way out of my drawers

I don't want to work today
I can't be arsed to clean my room
And I won't be jumping in the shower soon
Routine will only make me low in mood
So I don't want to work today

It's too much stress
To make my bed
You think I want to work today?
You're sick in the head!

I'm happy to lose track of time
Sip tea and be lazy even though I'm not tired
Because I don't want to work today
My hair needs brushing
I have spots that need popping
But I ain't rushing
So don't try to push me

I haven't done my homework
My friends have left me lonely
I don't give a fuck
So long as I don't have to work today

DON'T COLOUR OUTSIDE THE LINES

I've always had high hopes
Despite not believing in myself
I climbed up all the ropes
Because I wanted to be the best

I've been winning awards
Signing contracts and then books
Finally somebody noticed me
Would it be better if they hadn't have looked?

Don't colour outside the lines
Glory should only go so far
Some stars commit suicide because
Success so soon can break your heart

I'm trying so damn hard
And now it's happening all at once
It's going at a million times an hour
I feel like saying "Fuck this, I'm done"

The duress upon my back
Just to keep a smile on my face
Just a quick one for the camera
But my home is a lonely place

I don't care much for myself
Though to my fans I am devoted
That poem that lifted everyone else's mood
Yes, it was me that wrote it

My friends and my family
These days I find myself running away
They're struggling to understand me
They can't see why I'm so ashamed

Now I'm earning gold
I can't grasp how I deserve it
All my life I was told
That I was utterly worthless

Sometimes I feel numb
Should I be sad or should I be happy?
I can't believe the difference and
This change overwhelms me

Why am I doing this to myself?
I have people I'm meant to inspire
Every day I beat myself up
And yet I'm meant to be an idol

It's that voice inside my head
And the reality of people's doubt
That kept me in a shell
But maybe that's how I attracted a crowd

You know what? Fuck all the haters
Because I am still beautiful
If a tortured girl like me can do it
Then my tortured fans can do it too

DOOR'S STILL STANDING

Still residing
In a mental asylum
There's no denying
I'm doing my nut in
Staff aren't listening
I'm getting pissed off
The door gets a kicking
And now I'm limping
I'm a big wimp
But the door's still standing
My toe is fractured
The door had the last laugh

EYESIGHT OBSERVATIONS

I can't see a thing
But their eyes are on me
No space to think
I can't even pray to my Guardian Angel
Be careful what I write
They're reading not only my poems
But my mind
I'm scared they'll restrain me
If I even consider suicide
I haven't tied
A ligature
Just leave me alone
I don't deserve this
Why? Why are they doing this to me?
It gives me headache
The thought that I can't think
Ironic...
...don't you think?

GIVE ME TIME

I know I write
Of suicide
But give me time
And I'll be fine
I won't die
If I can help it...
All these rhymes
I speak my mind
Though some of the time
I fall out of line
These traits of mine
I'm not alone...
I often wonder why
So cruel is life
For the people who try
The hardest to survive
I'm one of that kind
You'll soon find
If I can continue to climb
And prove that I am worthy too

GOBBLE-DEE GOOK

I have writer's block
Yet I want to pass the time
So let's talk gobble-dee gook
See if we can make a rhyme

Quack, quack, miaow, miaow
Ruff, ruff, roar, roar
Eek, aah…careful! Ouch!
I dropped my knickers on the floor

Please don't pinch my eyelids
I'll have you know it really hurts
Did you know I'm going to win
A Christmas card this year?

My DVD player isn't working
I'll try banging it on my head
My pet lobster's been sunbathing
Oh no! My lobster has gone red!

Three sugars in my tea, please
That should quench my libido
Leave the teabags on the ceiling
And let's all do the limbo

A six-foot midget, he said to me
"I'm going to bend down and bite your nipples"
I know this dwarf, his name is Nelly
And he just wants a tickle

I've had an argument with my toenail
It says it hates to be chewed
But out of all your nails
Which one would you choose?

My Uncle can suck his own dick
He never leaves the house
He likes to drink his fresh piss
Which is why he has ulcers in his mouth

Well, time is useful and I'm getting older
My children all have beaks
I carry my kids on all three shoulders
It keeps them all happy

My phone keeps ringing – who could it be?
I suppose I've got another bill to pay
Nope, it's UK Book Publishing
"Stop talking shit!" is what they say

So, gobble-dee gook was fun
At least while it lasted
The only problem now is that
My book company think I'm a madhead

I DON'T GIVE A DAMN

I don't give damn if I step in dog shit
I don't care if my Mom puts the phone down on me
I don't give a fuck if I'm diagnosed with gonorrhoea
I don't give a shit if I break my middle finger

I don't give a damn if my taxi comes thirty minutes late
I don't care if my cigarette melts in the rain
I don't give a fuck if I drop my favourite mug on the floor
I don't give a shit if my leather sofa gets ripped

I don't give a damn if my most treasured CD gets scratched
I don't care if my bank card gets blocked
I don't give a fuck if the battery runs out of my remote control
I don't give a shit if the shower stops working
THESE are the least of my worries – I have a SOCIAL WORKER controlling my
entire fucking life (she's not that bad, I suppose)

I QUESTION

Sick with depression
I've got another headache
My hands are sweating
The point of life I question
This poem won't be inspiring
Because I'm feeling suicidal
I tell everyone I'm fine but
I want this day to be my final
Feeling like I want to slit my wrists
Or drink a pint of bleach
People tell me to snap out of it
The point of this I quiz
I've ruined my fucking life
Because I pulled out a knife
I'm being pushed to the limit
I don't want to live another minute

The belt of my night gown
Is calling me to it
I know what I want
But I bet both heaven and hell would turn me away

*(By the way, I'm an atheist, so life AND death I question.
I wish I hadn't been born at all. Thanks a lot, Dad)*

INSECURITY

I hate that I'm not confident
I detest that I can't always be what they want
I resent my vulnerability
And all my negativity
I despise how I always put others before me
And I abhor how much I absolutely abhor me

I fear that I'm not good enough
I'm afraid that I'm not tough enough
I'm frightened I'll never be loved enough
I'm scared one day I'll say "I've had enough"

All it takes is for my Mom to turn me away
And for my Dad to tell me that of me he's ashamed
How much longer can my best friend put up with me?
Or am I worrying unnecessarily?

Would I feel better if I had that bit of reassurance?
Problem is, nobody seems to want to say it for me
I write all these poems and yet I'm still insecure
I put my soul on to paper and worry all the more
I can never get any sleep at night
I stay in my room all day because I don't want to be seen in the light
Within these four walls all there is is a bed
A journal, a scrap book and a pen
This is all I can count on to survive

I can't help myself but compare and despair
Have I got what it takes to make it out there?
Maybe not...
...Then what?
Pointless counting sheep
I failed my only dream

Still, if staff didn't leave me in my room for so long
Without talking to me to see what's going on
Potentially I'd be able to explain myself
THAT I FEEL LIKE FUCKING KILLING MYSELF!!!

IT'S OVER

Headlining news: The coronavirus
An unwelcome and lethal present from China
Shops have shut down
There's nobody on the town
This curse is killing the population
We've all been told to stay in isolation
Could it get any worse?
Is this the end of the world?
Please somebody help us
We've done nothing to deserve this
Now thousands have an illness
That cannot be reverted
Selfish hoarders leaving the poor without food
You're out of work and so you're not getting paid
Schools are closed, there's kids that can't do their exams
And the government can't stick to a good enough plan
You can't accompany a sick person in hospital
So therefore we must all die alone
I may be thinking too far ahead
But I'll say it now before the end
It's over...corona

ITCHY MUFFIN

I turn around
Luckily nobody is looking
I stick my hands down my pants
And scratch my muffin
The only problem
I find with waxing
Is when it starts to grow back
It feels like cacti
Men are jealous
'Cos girls can fart out of there vaginas
Females are jealous
'Cos we have to keep our bits tidy
Some people get crabs
Some people have cobwebs
But I can't remember
The last time I received head
Oh, actually, yes I can!
It was absolutely appalling
And to all the other muffins he's licked
I feel sorry for them
I suppose sometimes they itch
'Cos they're longing for sex
But me, all I want is my nails
In between my legs

JEALOUSY

You called yourself a friend
Your words of support were bent
Inside you wished the worst for me
Because of one word; JEALOUSY
I can make it big without you
I can make it rich without you
Don't think that I will fail
Just because of your lack of faith
If at first I don't succeed
I'm sure that you'll be pleased
But I can destroy your happiness
When I reach platinum on my second attempt
I did this shit without you
Your expectations were completely untrue
Who are you to dictate my future?
Well, you were wrong and that's the beauty

KIND REGARDS

Always remember
The last hurdle is the hardest
'Cos one mistake
And then you're back to where you started
It's like one step forward
And two steps back
It's double the trouble
To get back on track
All it takes
Is a suicide note left on the desk
Too much attention
As if you're not already depressed
If all you want
Is a quiet and peaceful mind
Just remember
That seeking help is not a crime

LET YOURSELF IN

Let yourself in
Too cool for school
Sex, drinking vodka and smoking draw
What is wrong with today's society?
I wasn't like them so they bullied me

But I don't want a baby
At fifteen years old
Just so I can fit into the mould
What is wrong with teenagers these days?
I was treated like a reject because I was gay

Just make sure
That your parents spoil you rotten
Wear a gold chain and you'll never be forgotten
What do they find so unacceptable about me?
If you're a goth you'll never get treated respectfully

Hold on to that thought
You'd better buy a tracksuit
And don't forget your fucking stinky attitude
Why do the "En vogue" get it so easy?
Well, I don't care if I'm not appealing

I'm ugly and proud
I'm doing my own thing
And with a pen in my hand there's no stopping me
They'll soon find out which one is in charge
Yes, it's me and they can kiss my arse

LIES

A typical child's fantasy
Where mermaids liaise, swimming in the sea
Unicorns walk on water
Humans are immortal
Santa comes down the chimney on Christmas Eve
Children never witness this but they're made to believe it
Lose a tooth
You'll have a pound under your pillow
For a fairy has come
She flew through an unbroken window
One for sorrow
Two for joy
Avoid a magpie if it's solo
Children's superstition
Parents fucking with their cognition
Tell them an apple a day
Will keep the Doctor away
For fuck sake, leave the kids alone!

LIP SERVICE

You know, some evenings I get lonely
Feeling like I need a butch bitch to hold me
At midnight I take a trip to Birdy's room
We're gonna engage in some good lip service soon
It doesn't take much convincing to make her boxer shorts drop
We both take it on turns to get on top
I stroke one side of her neck with one hand and bite the other
And then her fingers start to wander
It's all foreplay and what's next I won't refuse
Because I know what she's been dying to do
Her pierced tongue where she wants it to be
I'm not complaining, she can have me for free
Multiple orgasms and heavy breathing from me
But she hasn't yet got what she wants from me
I'll serve her like a priority
Using my fingers and mouth simultaneously
Covered in cum, yeah we'll both get plastered
A new bedsheet? Nah, she'll need a new mattress
Staff are wondering where I've gone missing
Crowding around Birdy's room, we've left them hanging
No cameras please and do not disturb
We're both too busy getting down to dirt
Her breasts feel so good in my hands
I've fucked her good, no wonder she's a fan
Me and Chloe the Bird, we make a good team
Putting all lesbian pornography to shame
Her clitoris, it looks so neat
Now I know where to go when I want something sweet
Her eyes, how they gaze into my own
She's totally won me over, hands down
Did you think I was girly? I can be one fucking rude bitch
And to all the straight chicks out there –
If you knew what went on with me and Birdy,
I can make you switch

(this poem is a joke, by the way)

LOVE

Be everybody's friend
Don't believe in revenge
Let go of all your grudges
Tell your family that you love them
Don't wish any evil
On any of your people
Support those in need
Every day, just one good deed
We should all stick together
And be there for one another
Life is too short for hatred
So let's hold hands and be united

MENTAL HEALTH IS ABOUT

…recovery
It's about ambition
It's about self-efficacy
It's about believing
It's about bravery
It's about confidence
It's about motivation
It's about inspiration
It's about determination
It's about ebullience
It's about liberation
It's about pride
It's about gratitude
It's about giving
It's about receiving
It's about success
It's about beginning
It's about conquering
Remember, once you've found those feet of yours
You will run, climb and never look or fall down. You made it!

NOT GOOD ENOUGH

I can't do this any more
I cry so much my eyes are sore
I've tried my best
But when all is said and done
I serve no purpose
Because I'm not good enough

I've given to the poor
Yet I'm not being helped myself
I've tried my best
To lick everybody else's wounds
I failed, I serve no purpose
I guess I'm not good enough

Only a little while more
People will forget my name
I've tried my best
To inspire everyone
But when all is said and done
I'm just not good enough

Soon the shelves will run out of space
My books will get burnt
I've tried my best
To be number one
But when all is said and done
I'm just not good enough

NOTHING MEANS NO-ONE

Nothing means no-one means no reason to live means kill myself means heartbreak for the rest of my family means they'll have nowhere to turn to when they can get no good advice from anywhere else which means no answers. No answers? Means what's the point? Means the point is of no use. We live in a world where there is no unity, nobody is of one, no equality in this game which means we will fall like dominos and be bruised, have broken bones but there is no hospitals because nobody is surviving with this coronavirus that has no limits and is creeping up on the population, an illness with no cure which means that people are losing their innocent lives. There is no help meaning "no help" means "nothing" is leaving us with "no-one".

NYSTAGMUS

        N   tag
        Ys   mus

  Is a   ition   e eyes
        Cond   of th

  Where   bou   like flies
           they   nce

       Then   alize
          You re

  You've   sed   line
        Mis   all the   s

(Caused by my anti-epileptic medication. I think I'm about to have a seizure)

ODD SOCKS

From the way in which I hold my knife and fork
To my odd socks and pierced cheeks
To dressing my teddies in babies clothes
Everybody wants to be like me

From my falling in love in all the wrong places
And my dislike for the TV
To wearing boxer shorts and a men's shirt to bed
Everybody wants to be like me

From my only bathing in the dark
And being a fan from music in the 80's
To moaning during the summer's heat
Everybody wants to be like me

From wearing a ring on every finger
(except one of my pinkines)
To constantly cracking my knuckles
Everybody wants to be like me

From my accent to my dyspraxia
And for my admiration for Dutch cheese
To dreaming of sharing a bed with Selena Gomez
Everybody wants to be like me

From clouring my nails with a pencil when I'm bored
To playing "Bohemian Rhapsody" on repeat
To failing to apply eyebrow pencil properly
Everybody wants to be like me

From leaving toothpaste in the sink
To farting fuck knows how many times an hour
From not being arsed to shave for a week
Everybody wants to be like me

From yearning for a talking robot for Christmas
To having three sugars in my tea
To having night terrors if I don't hold my teddy at night
Everybody wants to be like me

From my pacing in circles and being fidgety
To accidently putting my phone in the washing machine
To losing my key when it's in my hand
Everybody wants to be like me

From falling asleep on the way home
Or simply being in a day dream
To trying to speak French when I'm shit at English
Everybody wants to be like me

From getting jealous of my ex-partners friends
To throwing wrappers on the floor when aiming for the bin
To compulsively buying books I'll never read
Everybody wants to be like me

From hanging my hand towel on my bathroom door
To soaking but never creaming my feet
To feeling like I owe the homeless money
Everybody wants to be like me

From leaving the lid off of the day's milk
To picking my nose when nobody is looking at me
From "forgetting" to flush the toilet (whatever!)
Everybody wants to be like me

From wanting a bigger bum so stuffing my face
And crossing the road when the traffic light is still green
From eating in bed and waking with a lollipop in my mouth
Everybody wants to be like me

From seeking sympathy over a bruise I caused myself
To flirting with men even though I don't find them sexy
From my fear of owls and my lack of excercise
Everybody wants to be like me

From staring into space, if that's what it called
To licking cotton buds before inserting them into my ear
From re-arranging my room every week
Everybody wants to be like me

Everybody wants to be like me
Let me tell you something sweet
I don't wish to sound cocky
But there's only one motherfucker like me

And that's me!

OESTROGEN

Eaten alive by oestrogen
I'm due my fucking period
It's that shitty time of every month
Where I become the embarrassment of Birmingham
Being a moody bitch and crying for no reason
Men just don't understand the feeling
It's the days where I bite, don't make me prove it
Mess with my hormones and your balls will be wounded
I'm just too damn emotional
I can't be helped by myself or anyone else
I have to wait a week to feel any better
Until then I just have to suffer
Yes, as I write this I'm a miserable twat
I'm trying to release stress but I can't relax
I've pushed all of my friends away
They wouldn't want to know me today anyway
It's not their fault, but is it really my own?
Nope, it's just the shit of being a woman

PAPA

Papa's getting older
Papa's lost a bone and
Paps had a diagnosis
Which turned out to be Myeloma

His wife broke down in tears
Papa had no fears
Though this cancer will not heal
Papa said "I'm not going anyhere"

How can he be so sure
When his illness has no cure?
Still this life he endures
Like he's only just been born

Papa walks with such pride
Such a legitimate design
Maybe he's in denial
In case panic cramps his style

If it was me that could die
I'd speed it up with suicide
Papa always finds a reason to smile, and
That's the Papa I admire

PATHOLOGICAL LIAR

Every might I cry when I'm given too much time to think
Whether the tears have meaning, I don't know, but I can't hold them in
Having a mental illness, you wouldn't believe the pressure
And my Dad thinks that I'm a pathological liar
I can't explain how much it hurts that he won't believe a word I say
I may as well do what I always did and talk to myself
Seems like I'm the only one that knows my history
Everything is distant in everyone else's memory
I'm not cruel enough to write exactly what I'm on about
Because I'm still trying to forget everything that happened back then
It's tearing me apart, who can I talk to other than my journal?
It's not as if I have a convinced family member to talk to
Daddy, don't you know how much it makes my heart ache
When you insist that all that comes out of my mouth is fake?
How do you think I feel knowing I can't confide in you any more?
All you want to ask yourself is how many more lies I have in store
Please put yourself in my shoes
Don't you think I'm lonely? You would be, too

PIGGY BACK

He comes up behind me
He places his hands on my shoulders
He puts all his weight on me
Then he leaps at me
I give Mr. Anxiety a piggy back
And he won't go away
I look straight ahead
I try to ignore it
But my face is blank
My eyes start to fill up
Please, Mr. Anxiety, leave me alone
Like a shadow
Is it my own?
Surely I wouldn't be so cruel to myself!
I'm not beating myself up
This came out of nowhere
It's not my shadow
This...
Is anxiety
For those of you that don't know

PLEASE DON'T CRY FOR ME

The beauty of your face
When a smile passes your lips
I never get to see it
Because you're always crying for me

When I sing a ballad
You forget the meaning of laughter
My poems go right through your skin
Darling, please don't cry for me

Stop beating yourself up
You have everybody's love
I'm not going anywhere
So you don't have to cry for me

You've always put others first
Despite your insecurity
Don't be afraid to be selfish
Baby, please don't cry for me

Your trauma and your paranoia
You keep locked inside your soul
Trust me, friend, I feel your pain, and
If you want to cry for me
At least shed a tear for yourself too

PRETTY GIRLS CRY TOO

I've straightened my hair and applied mascara
I've put lipstick on to make me feel better
Even if I did look pretty
Pretty girls cry too
I've left the top button of my shirt open
But all this false confidence is hopeless
Even if I did look pretty
Pretty girls cry too
I had a terrible dream last night
There's no denying that I look tired
And even if I did look pretty
Pretty girls cry too
People say "What's the matter with you? Don't you know you're beautiful?"
But what they don't understand is
That pretty girls cry too

PUT ON HOLD

My life's been put on hold and I'm losing faith
Why must everything have to wait?
There's no denying
That I've been crying
I don't think I want to play this game

I've been sitting in silence and losing patience
I put myself into this situation
Seems like I always fuck up
Cause nothing but tumult
All the dreams I have remain in the distance

I feel overwhelmed and I'm losing track of time
I hate the duress of sitting in front of amber lights
Turn green, turn green!
Let me pick up the speed
I can't be stunted; surely you must know me by now

Being kept on strings, fuck, I'm losing sanity!
You think I'm a puppet – don't patronize me
If you let me run
I can outshine the sun
Because when I take the brakes off there's no stopping me

ROBOTIC

The staff are robotic
Pay rent in the office
Glued to the computer
Absolutely fucking useless
They won't listen to us any more
It's always "Get out and shut the door!"
Fuck 'em, then

No time for the patients
They wonder why we get frustrated
And they're always moaning!
At least they have a home to go to
Where's their fucking restrictions?
No wonder I'm bitching…
Fuck 'em

The staff are robotic
Why do you think we've got problems?
It's the same old shit
Never mind, I'm used to it
After twelve years not a thing has changed
Well, I'm glad they earn their wage
Fuck 'em

The staff are robotic
They're always talking bollocks
The only time they get off their arses
Is when there's a fight in the garden
But I bet it makes them smug
That barely any of us get on
So fuck 'em

RUN AWAY FROM ME

No, I don't want to watch a film
I can't be arsed to run a bath
I can't find music to match my mood
Not much more to offer other than that...

Am I just being stubborn?
Sometimes I hate even my own company
I stick my nose up at myself
I wish I could run away from me

Go away reflection
But take me out the way, too
I can't decide which one I hate more
Out of me or you

SAME OLD SHIT

The tap won't stop running
Even though I turned it off
It's been like this
Ever since I brushed my teeth
Me, whilst my mind wanders
You know what I'm capable of
Maybe the tap is saying
I haven't brushed them properly
I moved from a sterile room
Only for this annoyance
Drip, drip, fucking drip
Yet the sink doesn't overflow
It doesn't matter how much I fume
I'm left with the same choices
It's the same old shit
Waiting for tomorrow
I can't see it from where I'm sitting
But the noise is monotonous
I tell invisible Lord "Thanks for this,
Now I'm absolutely pissed!"
Tap, stop fucking dripping!
The stress I keep bottled up
I feel like I want to bang my head
On the toilet next to it
Bang, bang, I'm out for the count
I bet the tap still won't relent
Now I have brain damage
But I can hear something
Dripping by the side of my head

SHOULD I?

All this negativity inside my head
Life is getting the better of me again
Should I wake?
Or should I sleep?
Should I carry on?
Or should I give up?
Is it relevant?
Should I ignore it?
Is it precious?
Or should I throw it all away?
Is it about me?
Or is it about you?
Should I have faith?
Could I ever turn Joey away?
Should I live?
Or should I take my own life?

SLAP IN THE FACE

…So you've got a problem with lesbians?
So you've got a problem with goths?
So you've got a problem with people's mental health?
Where the fuck did you come from?

Good luck if you think that you can change us
We're not going anywhere
It's pointless trying to under-rate us
We're too damn proud to care

All these labels, all these slights
Fuck you, we don't give a shit
Because of you it's not been an easy ride
But because of you our skin is thick

You think it's funny how we've had breakdowns
Just because it hasn't happened to you yet
Don't laugh too hard because your time will come
It will be the biggest slap in the face you'll get

Once you get there and suffer discrimination
I may have some sympathy for ya
Then you'll see for yourself what happens
When you have a mental health disorder

SLEEP PARALYSIS

I was eleven years old when I started to fall off the track
I can't emphasize how much I want my sanity back
Sometimes there's nothing better to do than gaze out the window
How I truly got myself into this mess, I don't know
Why can't I shake it off? Come on, I'm a poet!
That doesn't make me any less lonely
Not everybody is blessed with this talent
But I don't know whether this skill makes me happy or saddened
Am I talented or am I just intriguing
Because I have a mental illness?
For all I know, maybe nobody is listening
My name could be on the shelves but everyone keeps missing it
I read other people's poetry but still I have my own style
I wonder if these poets are taking a peek at mine
Have I just got too much a lack of confidence?
Or am I still too used to suffering in silence?
I try to speak but it feels like I have sleep paralysis
In these cold days the public eye is all I want for Christmas
I just had a dream where I was making a speech
It turned into a nightmare when not a sound came out of me
The audience was disgusted at me, the supposed "idol"
And when I woke I cried as I felt I'd lost everything I'd fought for
Please somebody, give me a voice
I think it's time I made some noise
Why is it that when I'm not asleep I'm still as reticent as if I was?
If I can't speak up for myself now then I may as well be shot
Get out of bed, I've got to do it some time soon
Before another victim of mental torture walks the street alone
I do apologize but I have a job to do
Who knows? The next person I save could be you

SLOB

I love my fans, i would do anything to make them happy
But apparently writing poetry isn't enough to make a living
For fuck's sake, i don't want to get a job!
Why can't i can be rich and yet still be a slob?
I'm getting five star reviews, isn't that enough?
Why can't i make a living out of selling books?
"No!" Dad says, "You must get a degree!"
I'm trying, man, i'm in university!
"You should be a professor of poetry"
I'd love to, but i'm too damn lazy
Doing my A-levels is such a drag
Essay after essay though so far, i've passed
I'm sick of my tutor, how does he sleep at night
Knowing he's the arsehole putting a burden on my life?
Right now i'm slouched on a cosy red beanbag
And leaving my last assignment for the last minute
Imagine ME in job interview?
I can't even pass an assessment for a lesser restrictive hospital!
Nobody would hire me, i'd just fall asleep driving to work
Because despite trying to motivate others...
...i'm a complete utter prick

SNIFF

I sniff socks
I sniff shoes
I sniff my Mom's favourite shampoo
I sniff paint
I sniff my shit
I sniff my sweaty armpits
I sniff flowers
I sniff chocolate
I sniff the fluff inside my pockets
I sniff mud
I sniff teddies
I sniff my dirty bedding
I sniff candles
I sniff earwax
Something about it helps me to relax
What a smell!
It's becoming unhealthy
Someone smother me before my nose falls off me!

SOFTEST APPROACH

My Guardian Angel tells me not to be vengeful
So some things I won't put to paper
I could be the most spiteful bitch in the world
But I'm just trying to keep others safer

My Guardian Angel tells me not to hate
So sometimes I have to bite my lip
For the record, I DON'T hate anybody
Yet I seem to be the only person feeling like this

My Guardian Angel says two wrongs don't make a right
And that is why I'm being benign
I try to think of the softest approach
Even if it stops me sleeping at night

My Guardian Angel tells me I must forgive
Though some people don't want to say sorry
I'm big enough to accept an apology
But I've never had one laid on me

My Guardian Angel tells me I must be strong
Never to let others defeat me
There's only so much that I will write but
Behind every poet there's a story

SOME WILLIES

Some willies are big
Some willies are small
Some willies are too scared to be explored
Some willies are impotent
Some an involuntary erection
Some willies are hungry
Some willies are asexual
Some know how to please
Some don't have a clue
But if you put your willy near me
Guaranteed it will be bruised

STERILE ROOM

They couldn't trust me
I tried to hide but I was busted
Caught in the act
Of me trying to punish me

They moved me to a sterile room
Not anything new
I've been here before
It won't lift me any time soon

Put on observations
I refused my medication
Red alert for them
They see I'm getting agitated

I've never felt so lonely
This place isn't homely
They say they're here to listen
But not a word comes out of me

I just want to sleep
Through the whole week I'm here
And thanks to this blip
I guess I'll be here another year

TEA STAIN ON THE DESK

Everything's out of my control
I've failed again
Not one for playing the perfect role
Of an inspiration
I'm sorry, I didn't mean to fuck things up
But I did
Things as usual got too much
So I slipped
Staff noticed my head was a mess
I had to move rooms
Nothing to look at but a tea stain on the desk
I can't be worthy
I didn't want this attention
I got it
Stuck on observations
No exit
All I wanted was to die in peace
Not if they have their say
I'm really not in the mood for this
It's written on my face
No bathroom privacy
What the - ?
Never mind my modesty
I'm all theirs
I stand right before their eyes
They STARE
I have no more to hide
I swear
Would they do this to an animal?
Then why an alien like me?
I know they have a job to do
But it's killing me
At least leave me in a clean domain

I deserve respect…don't I?
The cleaners haven't done their job properly
And that's why
They've thought nothing of the tea stain on the desk

TELL THE NURSE

Tell the nurse you need lorazepam
You'll lose your leave for the following day
Tell the nurse you feel like slitting your wrists
Sooner than you know, your room gets stripped
Tell the nurse you're having hallucinations
Then she'll increase your observations
Tell the nurse that you're depressed
She'll bring you rip-proofs and tell you to get undressed
Punch the nurse in the face
You'll get pinned down and acufased
Nothing is easy in a psychiatric ward
All the nurse wants between you and her is war

THE GHOST IN MY ROOM

There's a ghost in my room
It steals my socks
It blocks my toilet
It hides my bus pass
It makes me wet the bed
It lets out stinky farts
It dyes my hair grey
It spills tea on the carpet
It leaves dirt on the rug
It spreads dust on my desk
It keeps leaving toothpaste in the sink
It kicks my teddies out the bed
It uses all my handwash
It ate my last biscuit
I'm SURE there was one left
Call the police, because at the moment
Everybody is blaming me

THE POEM THAT WAS TORN

The poem that thought you were my friend
The poem that thought I was friendly with you too
It's been torn
Because I no longer love you

The poem that thought you cared
The poem that thought I cared for you too
It's been torn
Because I no longer love you

The poem that thought you'd always be there
The poem that thought I'd be there for you too
It's been torn
Because I no longer love you

The poem that thought I was your soulmate
The poem that thought you were precious to me too
It's been torn
Because I no longer love you

The poem that thought I was blessed
To have you in my life
It's been torn
And it's the best thing I've done tonight

Now I can sleep easy
Knowing there's no compliments for you
It's all been torn
Because I no longer love you

THE TWINS OF BANGLADESH

Two gorgeous women and only one personality
The actresses of my sexual fantasies
Long black hair and a beautiful olive complexion
Scented perfume drawing me closer to them
I know there would be a plan for safeguarding
If staff knew how I felt about their colleagues
But every time the twins of Bangladesh pass me by
My perverted thoughts race and I can't help but smile
Man, I look at them and I can't think of another subject
They're so damn hot – I think I'm obsessed
All I talk about is how much I fancy them
It saddens me that I don't stand a chance with them
One of them, she winks at me
Hey! That's not fair, she's teasing me!
Well, unless she wants to miss out on a lot of fun
She'd better become a lesbian
Maybe I could kick off and be put on observations
And then when I get one of the twins I can lie there masturbating
Please, what in the world would it take of me
To have the twins of Bangladesh in bed with me?

THE WAY OUT

I promise I'll take my medication
I promise I'll keep away from danger
I promise I'll engage in social services
I promise I'll pay attention to financial awareness
I promise I'll stay away from alcohol
I promise I'll find a decent job
I promise I won't steal
I promise I won't end up in jail
I promise I won't do drugs
I swear I won't give up
I promise I won't be violent
I promise I'll tell someone if I feel suicidal
I promise I won't talk to strangers
Just let me pack my things and show me the way out

THIS VOICE

This voice inside our heads
We bang our heads to get it out
But it only makes this voice angry
And then it starts to shout
This voice is telling us we're ugly
This voice is telling us we're weak
This voice is telling us to hurt ourselves
But we must not let this voice defeat

I'm talking from experience
I've cut, ligatured, overdosed and punched walls
That cryptic voice inside my skull
Was the only reason I did it at all
I've been told a thousand times I'm worthless
By who? Not my friends or my parents
Of course, it's this voice that I have to deal with
This voice that doesn't seem to go away any further

The doctors have kept me medicated
They can't see the futility
I've tried telling them that I still struggle with this voice
This voice that nobody else can see
Anybody else out there that hears a voice?
A voice too scared to physically come out and play?
Boy, if this voice was brave enough to show up
I'd tear up it's fucking face!

How dare this voice tell me that I'm a retard
Just because I have psychosis?
Every day I'm faced with another
Sack of convolution
I cry at night when I'm left alone
And given too much time to think
These thoughts wouldn't even be there at all
If it wasn't for this voice and how it always wins

We all know we can't run away
From this voice that seems to take over
But we can do a million things that this voice can't
So why should we let this voice make us suffer?
This voice will visit us time and again
Sometimes more than often
Let's not forget that we have a voice too
Don't let that voice make you a target

UNIVERSITY

The place of mental torture
Intimidated by the tutor
So many books to read
That will mean nothing in a decade
Too scared to ask a question
But you must pass this season
The financial black hole
Though you're living on the dole
You're only looking to succeed
Never thought it would come to this
So much fucking stress
You want to bang your head on the desk
Must be easy for a model
So long as you're pretty, no problem

Sooner than you know
You're doing your exams
The tutor watches over
Standing in front of the class
So confused
You can't even remember which hand you write with
Nothing runs smooth
You've never been so frightened
Last sentence, hand it in
The tutor takes it with a grin
Surely they don't want us to fail, right?
At least you can rest assure you tried
Six weeks later, you get your feedback
The tutor says you've done fantastic
There you go, you've got your grades
Better celebrate with a glass of ale!

WASHING MACHINE

Every Monday and Thursday of every week
My dirty clothes are escorted for a clean
You think my bed shirt likes to sweat?
Wait until I take it to the launderette!
I open the washing machine door, in they go
There's nothing my socks hate more
Than having a soak
The button is pressed
My bra gets stressed
"Help us!" scream my boxer shorts
Part of me feels utterly cruel
My hoody feels despondent of my jogging bottoms
I tell it they're coming in my second load of washing
Round and round, I watch them spinning
I suppose they're used to it, but me, I'd be dizzy
An hour later they're ready to come out
I'm expecting a bollocking from my dressing gown
Look, guys I'm sorry, but it has to be done
I understand you get claustrophobic but now at least you smell good
Oh, shit – that's where I left my keys!
I find them in the pocket of my jeans
I'm just like my late Nan
Anyway – you fuckers are going in the dryer, that should give you something to cry
about, right T-shirt?

WE

We are incompetent
We are special
We are unique
...but we are equal

WHERE DID THE MONEY GO?

I left the lid off of my bank account open, and
An advisor told me that I'd spent thousands!
Silly me, I just wasn't used to being rich
All, that money, what was I supposed to do with it?
At least I can say that I have given to the homeless
Problem is now I've left myself almost broken
My Grandparents left me the inheritance to start a new chapter
And then I blew it all like I was a rock star
Fourteen weeks I spent nearly £3,000 – or is that average?
Plus I spent £1,450 to get my first book on the market
Man, I hope my writing pays me back well
Because it looks like I'm digging my way into hell
Do authors know that Amazon take 40%
Of every book printed on demand?
Still, where would I be without these wholesalers?
It's the only way I can attempt to be famous
Guess I'll probably end up going back to prostitution
Unless I get off my arse here and get an education
(At least that got me thinking – I want to be a professor of poetry)

WORN OUT

Woken up for medication at nine o' clock
Something's up with me but I don't know what
I look in the mirror, I look a disgrace
Bags under my eyes and spots all over my face
The cleaners come around, bless, I know they only want to help
But I tell them to fuck off and say I'll do it myself
I've left my bedroom a mess until I can't take it any more
Then it's time to make my bed and vacuum the floor
Pushing that bastard thing around, it's such a drag
Same shit, different day and it's driving me mad
I can't work out whether I'm depressed or just worn out
Either way, I don't seem to be laughing now
This daily routine, I don't want to be bothered
Still I have no choice even if I don't like it
People think I'm okay because I don't have to pay gas or electric
Though would you rather be sane, or like I'm getting – MENTAL!!!
For fuck's sake, this place is no hotel
In fact it's the closest you'll get to hell (If not, worse)
I should know, I've been detained for thirteen years
Even when I was in prison I was better off there
Staff just sitting on their arses pretending to be busy
Too busy to attend to patients when all they want is somebody to listen
I'm sick of this bollocks, why can't the doctor set me free?
Oh, because I'm a danger to society
Stop dwelling on my past, I'm a changed person now
I'm not a fucking psychopath
JUST LET ME THE FUCK OUT!!!!!!

YOU KNOW WHO YOU ARE

I fell in love
With a narcissist
He was the proud possessor of the arse I licked
Strange how it happened
It's not like me
Craving a man like I did was out of the ordinary
But he was so gorgeous
At least for a guy
Until I worked out his personality
Six foot three inches tall
Seductive brown eyes
It took me over a year to see through his lies
All I craved was him
To hold me close
All he cared about was his boosted ego
He liked to boast
About the drugs he took
And all the prostitutes he'd allegedly fucked
Still, I've heard some rumours
Even got him to admit
That these days he struggles to work his dick
Medication, maybe?
So, he's not so perfect
Any other man would be fine without it
I have low self-esteem
That he took advantage of
Why couldn't I see that he was leading me on?
There's no denying
That when I worked him out
I wish I would have just closed my mouth
I was always telling him
About how I truly felt
Looking back all I can do is regret
He seemed to think
That he was too good for me

I don't think so, but he makes me write good poetry
And yes, before he asks
This one is for him
He knows exactly who he is if he's reading this
I don't see his signature
On the front of a book
So who's gone down and who's going up?
Needless to say
I'm better off without him
Because all he lives off is his vanity
One quick reminder
I'd like to say
Big-heads don't go far, even with a pretty face

YOU'RE NOT ALONE

I was diagnosed with psychosis at thirteen years old
The lack of support was what hurt me the most
So scared to open up, I was in denial
But this time you won't keep me quiet
Now, I'm not hungry to be famous
I just want to make a statement
Sell my rhymes and make myself heard
I've already got a fanbase, spread the word
Here's to all of you that are being discriminated
You mustn't feel like you are alienated
Don't worry, guys, I've got your back
Never let anyone cut you slack
I may sound like a hero but I can't do this on my own
Just remember you're not alone
I've been in services and behind bars
But I'm not at all frightened to reveal my scars
Every time I cut I know I'm bleeding for us
Because the stress we have to go through is too much
We should all stick together and be there for each other
Rather than keeping our heads hidden under the cover
I know we can do this, look how far we've come
The fact that we are still breathing should say it all
I admit I've tried to end my life
Though secretly I didn't really want to die
All I wanted was a helping hand
And now I'll be the helping hand to those in demand
My aim is to be an inspiration
To all of those in isolation
Come out of your shells and scream if you want to
Because the world needs proof of what we really can do

Printed in Great Britain
by Amazon